Mel Bay Presents

Mastering the Guitar

A COMPREHENSIVE METHOD FOR TODAY'S GUITARIST!

CLASS METHOD

Level 2

By William Bay &
Mike Christiansen

(For Note Review see page 167 and for Chord Review see page 168.)

Complete lesson plans availible on the internet go to:
www.guitarpeople.com/teachers then proceed to downloads.

This book is available either by itself or packaged with a companion audio and/or video recording. If you have purchased the book only, you may wish to purchase the recordings separately. The publisher strongly recommends using a recording along with the text to assure accuracy of interpretation and make learning easier and more enjoyable.

1 2 3 4 5 6 7 8 9 0

Visit us on the Web at www.melbay.com — E-mail us at email@melbay.com

Table of Contents

Key of C Review
Aura Lee

Civil War Song

Slowly

The Riddle Song

Moderately

Key of C

Jacob's Ladder

Slowly

Spiritual

Arkansas Traveler

Allegro

Cruisin' Sunset

Moderately, let notes ring

MC

Springtime

Arr. by Mel Bay

Guitar Duet

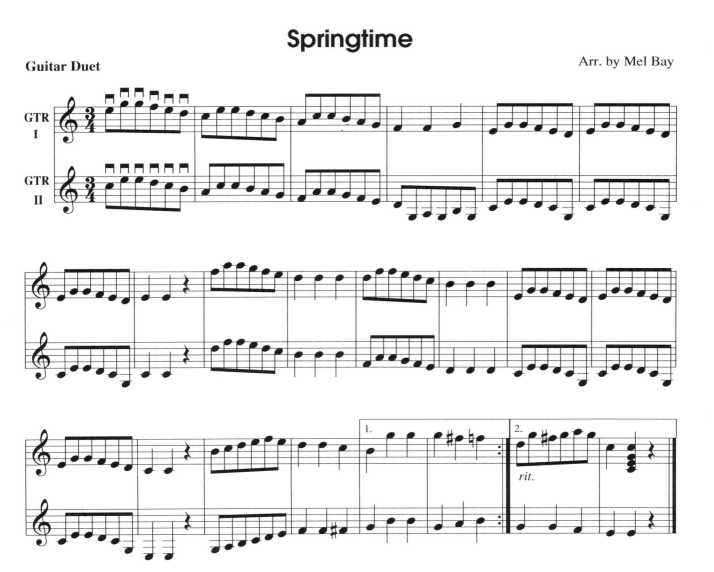

Separate Paths

Guitar Duet

Moderato

PLEYEL
Arr. by Mel Bay

Key of C

Play to the end, then without a break in the rhythm, play the piece backwards to the beginning. After playing the piece backwards, play the final note twice.

Reversible Duet

Al Rovescio

Flyin' South
(Reggae Feeling)

Key of C

Song Without Words

Guitar Duet

Arr. by Mel Bay

Key of G Review
Darling Nellie Grey

Stephen Foster

Key of G

Toll Free

MC

Gavotte en Rondeau

Guitar Ensemble

Allegro

Dandrieu

Key of G

Devil's Dream

Key of G

Gavotte

This piece is a duet. Half the class plays the duet as written. The other half turns their books upside down and plays the duet starting at the "end." The two parts harmonize one another.

Moderato   Anon.

Key of G

Minor Seventh Chords

The following are popular minor seventh chords in first position. Practice changing from one chord to the next. Then, practice the exercises written below the diagrams.

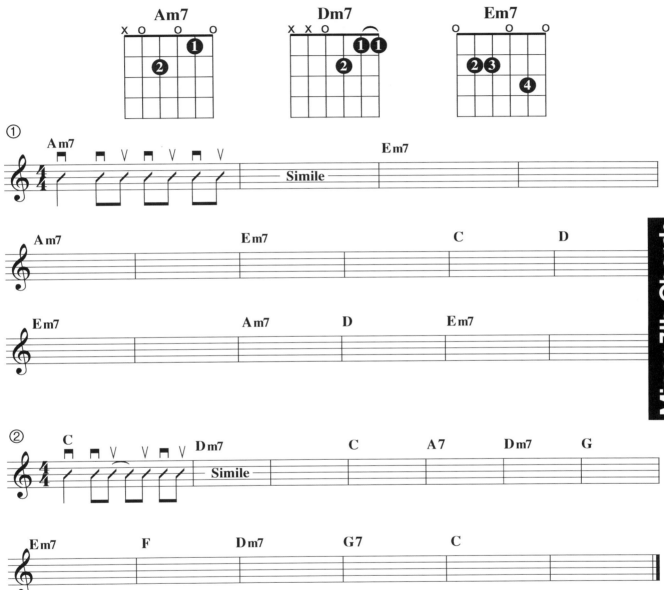

Minor 7th Chords

Major Seventh Chords

Drawn below are some popular major seventh chords in first position. Major seventh chords may be written as Maj7, △, or $\overline{7}$. Practice changing from one chord to the next. Then, practice the exercises written below the diagrams.

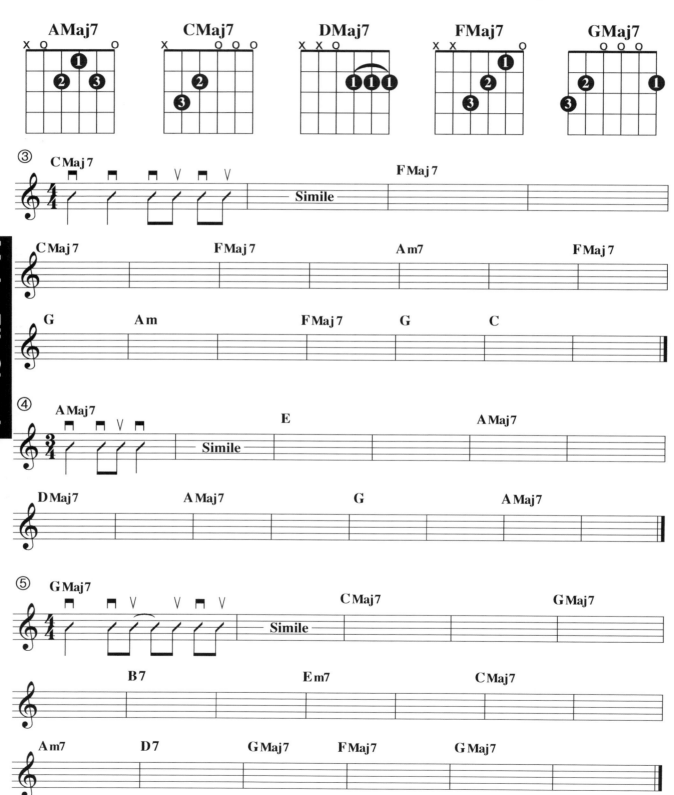

Major 7th Chords

Dotted Quarter Review

 = One and 1/2 counts

Auld Lang Syne

The Ship that Never Returned

Dotted Quarter Review

Rondo

Guitar Duet

MAZAS, Op. 85
Arr. by Mel Bay

Dotted Quarter Review

Syncopation Review

Syncopation means placing the accent on a beat (or part of the beat) which is normally weak. Syncopation is often done by playing a note on the up beat (second half of the beat, or the "and") and letting that note ring through the first half of the next beat. Syncopated rhythms are commonly written as a quarter note or quarter notes between two eighth notes. Sometimes the second eighth note is replaced by a dot after the quarter note. The following illustrations show how syncopated rhythms are written and how they are counted. Some of the songs, exercises, and solos in this book contain these rhythms. It's important that you understand how they are counted. Hold any note and practice tapping your foot on the beat while you play and count aloud the rhythms written below.

Practice the following exercises and song which contain **syncopation**.

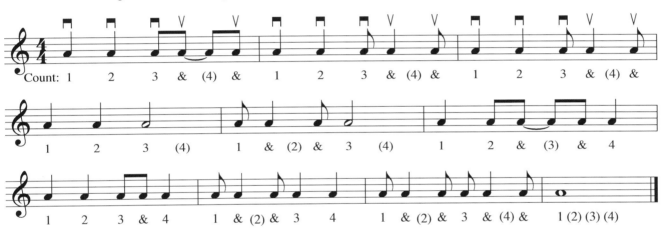

Play the following piece which contains syncopation.

Tango For Edgar

Syncopation Review

Rise and Shine

Lively Tempo

Spiritual

Sambolêtê

Moderately

Brazilian

Key of A Minor Review

There are no sharps or flats in the key of A minor. A minor is "relative" to the key of C.

Arcadian Melody

God Rest Ye, Merry, Gentlemen

Na Pali Coast

The numbers written next to the notes in the following piece are suggested left-hand fingerings.

Anitra's Dance Theme

Trio from Divertimento III

Key of A Mino
Review

D.S. (𝄋) al Fine

When this phrase appears at the end of a piece (**D.S 𝄋 al fine**) go back to the sign (𝄋) and play until you see the word **"Fine,"** which means "The End"

Menuet

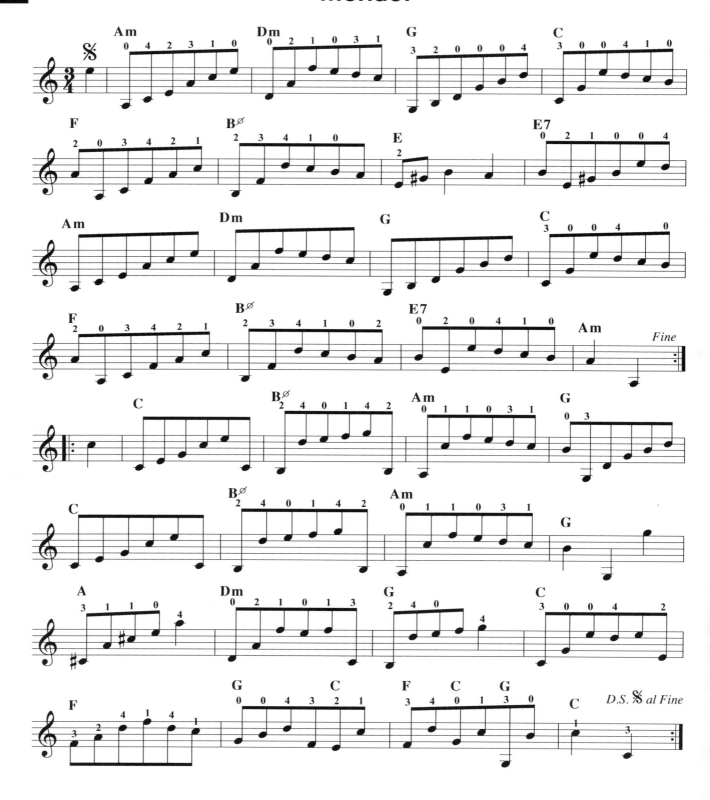

Triplets

A **triplet** is a group of three notes played in the time of two notes of the same kind.
An eighth note triplet () gets one beat if the bottom number in the time signature is a four.

Say: one Trip-let *or* Am-ster-dam

When using a pick, eighth note triplets are generally picked down-up-down.

Blues for Tuesday

Triplet Blues

Triplet Duet

Moderato

Mel Bay

Swing Rhythm

Normally when two eighth notes are connected together (♫) the beat is divided into two equal parts. When playing jazz and blues, it's more common to use **swing rhythm**. This means the first eighth note is longer than the second, so the beat is divided into a long-short pattern. With swing rhythm, two eighth notes are written the same but they are interpreted and played as a one-beat triplet with the middle note tied (♫ = ♪♪♪). Often, if the piece is to be played with swing rhythm this ♫ = ♪♪♪ will be written at the beginning of the music. Sometimes swing rhythm is also referred to as **shuffle rhythm**. To get the swing feel, practice playing a single note over and over as in the example written below. First, play the eighth notes even then swing them.

Next, practice playing the following scale and swing the eighth notes.

The rhythm will swing even more if you accent the off-beats. The example below shows where the accents would occur. Notice the accents come on the upstroke.

Another technique used to make the music swing and have a better jazz feel, is to accent the notes which precede and follow rests. The example below shows where these accents would be placed.

Practice playing the following blues solo and swing eighth notes.

I Don't Know Why

Swingin' the Changes
Guitar I
(Conductor's Score Found on Page 151)

Guitar Ensemble – GUITAR I

Swingin' the Changes

Swingin' the Changes
Guitar II
(Conductor's Score Found on Page 151)

Swingin' the
Changes

Swingin' the Changes
Guitar III
(Conductor's Score Found on Page 151)

Swingin' the Changes

Swingin' the Changes
Guitar IV
(Conductor's Score Found on Page 151)

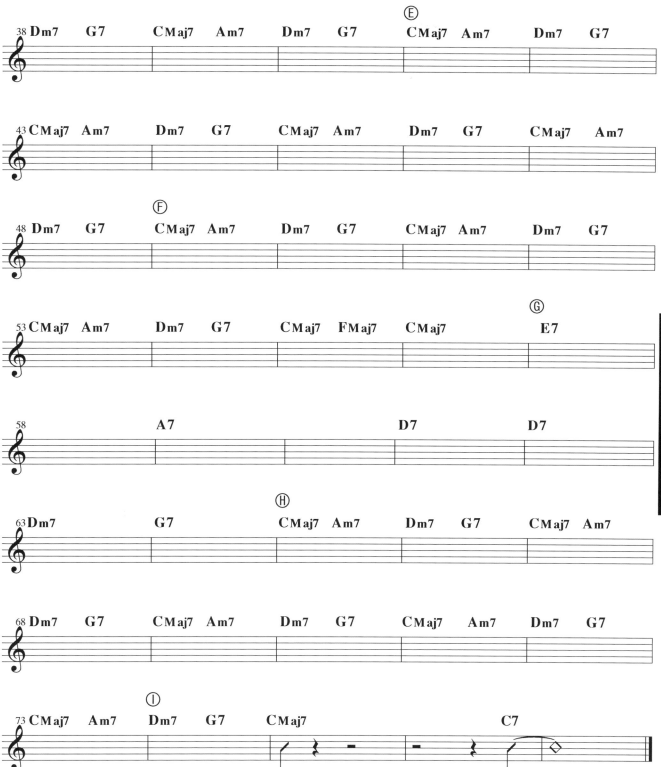

Swingin' the Changes

Jimmy's Shuffle
(Swing Feeling)

Heavy Weight
(Swing Feeling)

Swing Rhythm

The Slide

A *slide* is indicated with a slanted line and an "*sl.*" written before a note. If the line slants up to the note, slide from two frets below to the written note. If the line slants down to the note, slide from two frets above to the written note. If two notes are connected with a slanted line, pick the first note and without picking the string again, slide the same finger on the string to the second note.

Slide Song

Slow Blues Feeling

At Midnight

Very slow, Bluesy

Slide Groove

Medium Tempo

The Slide

Acoustic Blues
Guitar I
(Conductor's Score Found on Page 154)

Guitar Ensemble – GUITAR I   ♩=92

indicates the piece is to be played using swing rhythm

MC

Section C is open for solos. Parts may be played as background, or Guitar IV may play power chords without the background parts.

Section C may be repeated as many times as desired.

Acoustic Blues

D.S. al Coda

Rest 8 measures

Multimeasure rest

Acoustic Blues

Acoustic Blues
Guitar II
(Conductor's Score Found on Page 154)

Guitar Ensemble – GUITAR II   ♩=92

indicates the piece is to be
played using swing rhythm

MC

Section C is open for solos. Parts may be played
as background, or Guitar IV may play power
chords without the background parts.

Section C may be repeated
as many times as desired.

Acoustic Blues

Rest 4 measures

Multimeasure rest

Rest 4 measures

D.S. al Coda

Acoustic Blues

Acoustic Blues
Guitar III
(Conductor's Score Found on Page 154)

indicates the piece is to be played using swing rhythm

Rest 2 measures

Multimeasure rest

Section C is open for solos. Parts may be played as background, or Guitar IV may play power chords without the background parts.

Section C may be repeated as many times as desired.

Rest 8 measures

D.S. al Coda

Acoustic Blues

Acoustic Blues
Guitar IV
(Conductor's Score Found on Page 154)

Acoustic Blues

E Minor Review

In the key of E minor there is 1 sharp in the key signature—F#. The key of E minor is the "relative" minor to the key of G major.

Minuet
(Duet)

WB
J.S. Bach

Six-Eight Time

This sign indicates six-eight time
6 —beats per measure
8 —type of note receiving one beat

An eighth note ♪ = one beat, a quarter note ♩ = two beats, a dotted quarter note ♩. = three beats, and a sixteenth note ♬ =1/2 beat. Six-eight time consists of two units containing three beats each. It will be counted: with the accents on beats one and four.

1 - 2 - 3 - 4 - 5 - 6

Here are two Irish jigs. Watch for the C♯ notes

Swallowtail Jig

Morrison's Jig

How Pleasant It Is to Dwell in Harmony

Six-Eight Time

6/8 and 12/8 Strums

Written below are the strum patterns which work for songs in **6/8** and **12/8** time. Hold any chord and practice these patterns.

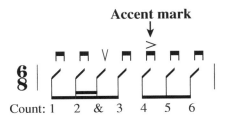

Accent mark

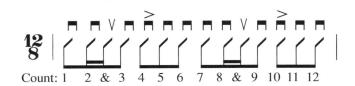

In 6/8 and 12/8 the eighth note strum ( ) gets one beat and the sixteenth note strum ( ) gets 1/2 beat

Practice the following progressions in 6/8 and 12/8. Use the strum patterns which are written in the first measure to play each measure of the progression.

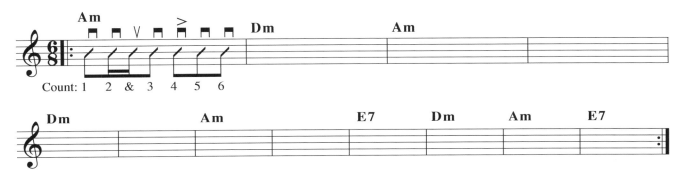

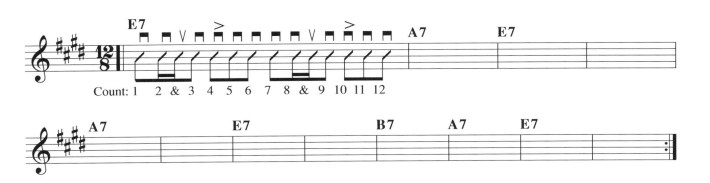

/8 and 12/8
Strums

Practice the following song using the strum for 6/8 which is written above the first measure.

House of the Rising Sun

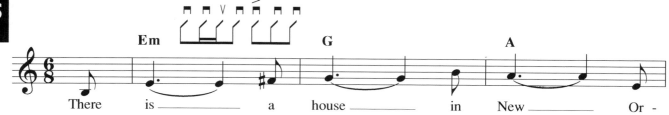

There   is —————— a   house ——— in   New ——— Or -

leans,——— they   call ——— the   ris   -   ing   sun.———

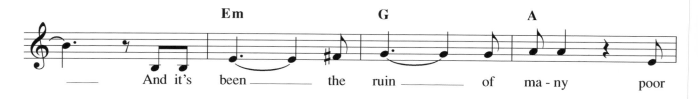

——— And it's   been ——— the   ruin ——— of   ma - ny   poor

boy,——— and   God——— I   know——— I'm   one.———

Harmonics

When a string is touched lightly in the correct spot, the vibration of the string is divided causing a "bell-like" tone. This is called a harmonic. One type of harmonic is called a "natural" harmonic. These natural harmonics occur in many places. Some of the more common natural harmonics are play in the 12th, 7th, and 5th frets. The 12th fret will probably be the easiest place to play a harmonic. A natural harmonic is played by **lightly** touching a left-hand finger **directly** over a fret wire and picking the string. In the 12th fret, use the left-hand fourth or third finger to touch the string. After picking the string, move the left-hand finger away from the string allowing the harmonic to ring.

Harmonics are written as diamond shaped notes (♦) and 'Harm.' is written above the note. The Roman numeral above the note indicates on which fret to play the harmonic. The circled number by the note shows on which string the harmonic is to be played. '8va' above or below a note means the harmonic will sound one octave higher than the note which is written.

In tablature, harmonics are written with a diamond around a number, or with a diamond written by the number.

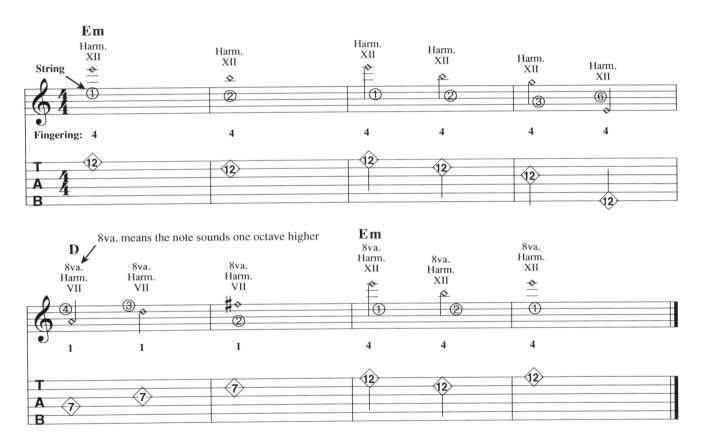

Harmonics

Danza

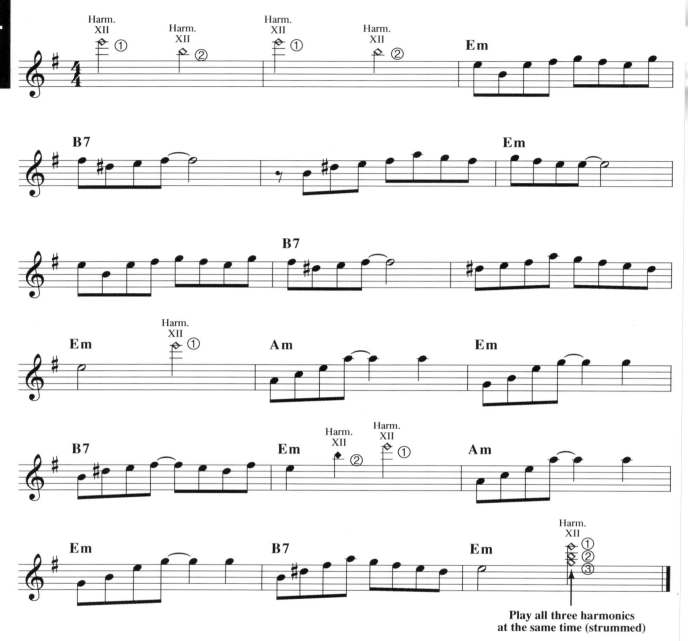

Play all three harmonics
at the same time (strummed)

Suspended (sus) Chords

Drawn below are some common suspended chords played in first position. Practice each chord and then play the exercises.

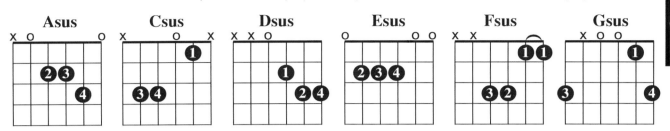

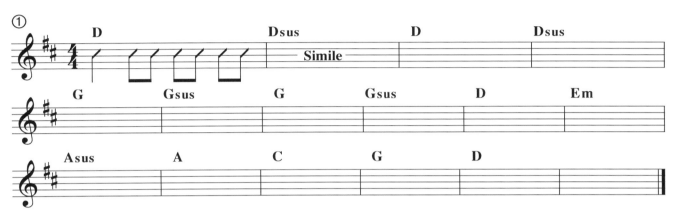

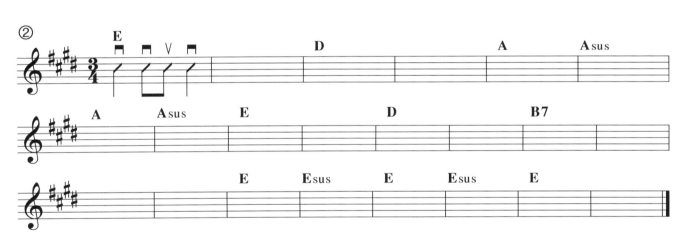

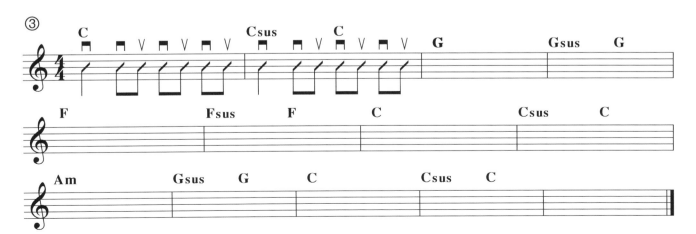

Suspended Chords

Moveable Power Chords

In order to play power chords other than A5, D5, and E5, open strings cannot be used. The diagram below shows a moveable power chord. It can be positioned anywhere on the guitar neck. When playing this chord, play only the strings which have fingers on them. The dot with the "R" pointing to it is the "root." The letter name of this note will be the letter name of the power chord. The chart below the diagram shows the names of the notes (roots) on the sixth string and the fret numbers in which they are located. By using the chart below and moving the power chord pattern, it will be possible to play 12 power chords.

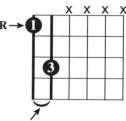

Indicates to play only strings six and five.

Sixth String Roots

Fret	0	1	3	5	7	8	10	12
Root name	E	F	G	A	B	C	D	E

Power chords may be played on any step of the scale. For example, B5 would have the root in the 7th fret.

B5

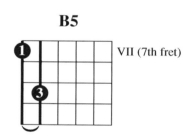

To sharp a power chord, move the pattern up one fret. To flat a power chord, move the pattern down one fret.

G♯5

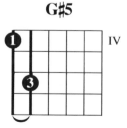

B♭5

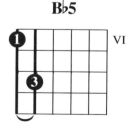

Practice the following exercises using power chords with the roots on the sixth string. Play down eight times in a measure (two times to a beat).

count: 1 & 2 & 3 & 4 &

Power chords may also be played with the root on the fifth string. The diagram below shows how this is done. The C5 power chord with the root on the fifth string is positioned so the finger on the fifth string is in the third fret (C).

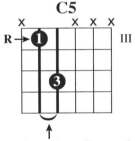

Play only strings five and four.

The chart below shows the locations of the note names (roots) on the fifth string.

Fifth String Roots

Fret	0	2	3	5	7	8	10	12
Root name	A	B	C	D	E	F	G	A

Moveable Power Chords

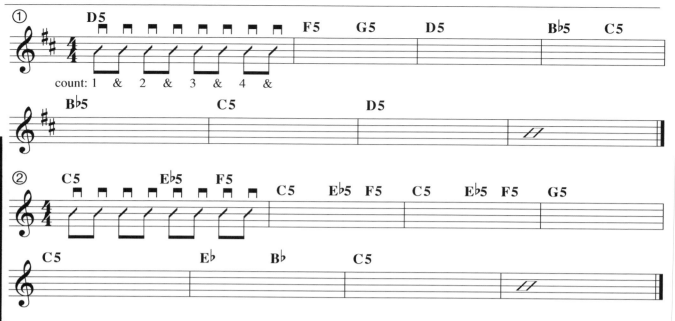

By combining power chords with their roots on the sixth and fifth strings, you can change chords and keep them positioned close to each other and avoid a lot of unnecessary position shifting.

Practice the next exercise using combinations of power chords with the roots on the sixth and fifth strings. To help you know which power chord to use, those which have their root on the sixth string have an "R6" next to them and those with their root on the fifth string have an "R5".

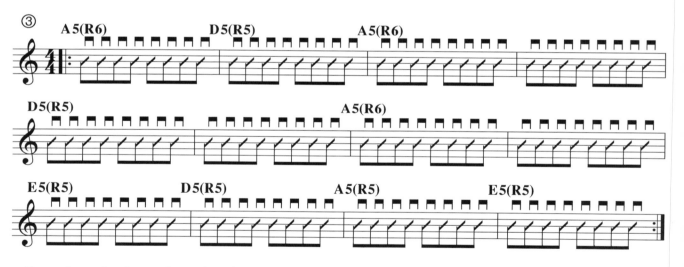

The next exercise also uses two categories of power chords. The E5 power chord in this exercise may be played using the sixth string open and the fifth string, second fret.

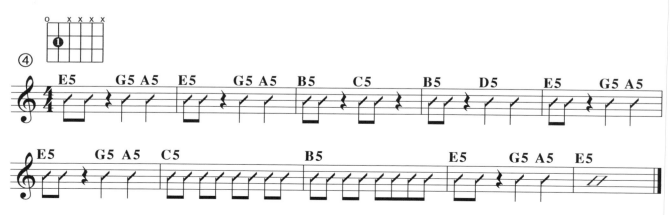

Play the next song using moveable power chords. Play each power chord eight times in a measure. The guitar part is written in tablature and the melody for the vocal part is written in standard notation.

I Left My Baby

Like the open string power chords, moveable power chords can be modified. This is done by playing the chord down four times, Be sure to play only the strings which have fingers on them. On the third stroke, add the left-hand fourth finger where the "X" appears on the diagram. Lift the fourth finger off on the fourth stroke. Do this two times in each measure. Use only down strokes. The diagram below shows how this technique is used on a power chord with the root on the sixth string.

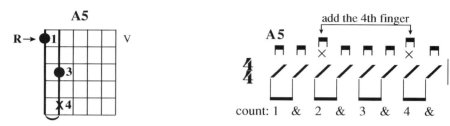

The following shows the notation and tablature for this technique for the A5 chord.

The next diagram shows how this technique would be used on a power chord with the root on the fifth string.

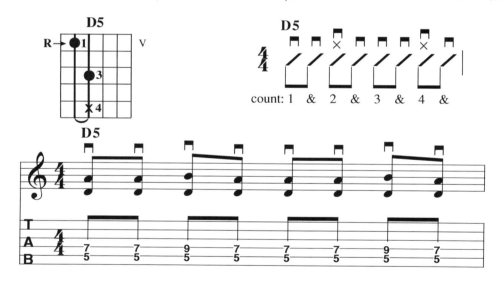

Practice the following exercises using moveable power chords with the variation. Try to keep the chords close to one another by using power chords with the roots an the sixth and fifth strings.

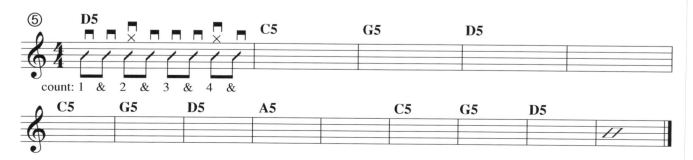

Moveable Power Chords

Play the following exercises using the variation in the moveable power chords.

Blues Power

Practice the following song using the variation on moveable power chords. The guitar accompaniment is written in tablature and the melody is written on the top line in standard notation.

Baby Don't Love Me

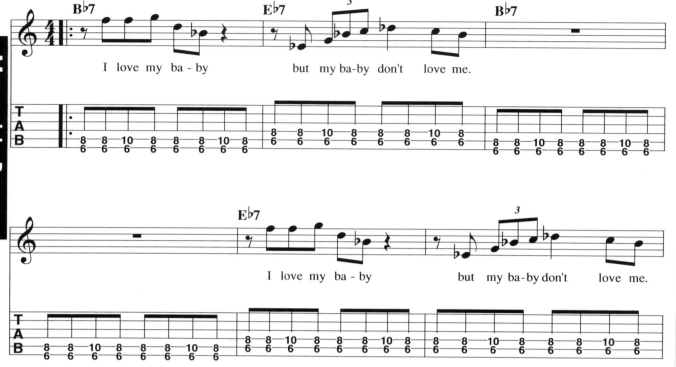

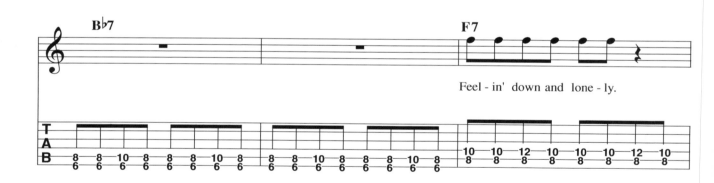

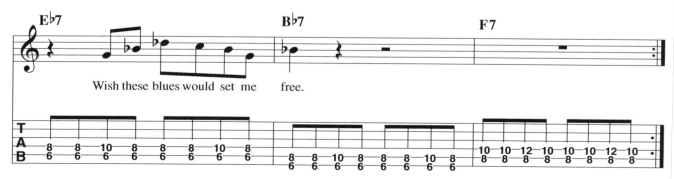

Key of D

In the key of D we have two sharps. They are F♯ and C♯.

D Scale

Velocity Study #1

Key of D

Velocity Study #2

Second Time Around

D.C. al Coda

When you see the marking D.C. al Coda, go back to the beginning and play until you see the To Coda and sign (𝄌). When you reach this point, skip down to the second coda sign or the ending.

D.C. al Coda

Texas Tea

Flatpick Solo
Smoothly, connected

Play slowly, keep your wrist loose.

Almost There

Dance

Guitar Ensemble
Allegro

John Dowland

D.C. al Coda

Dance from the Spanish Renaissance

Guitar Ensemble ♩=108

Gaspar Sanz

Rhythmically

D.C. al Coda

Cut Time
(Alla Breve)

The sign for cut time is **¢**. This means to count each measure in 1/2 the time. Thus:

Cuckoo's Nest

Eighth of January

* High B is played on the 1st string, 7th fret

A Minor Pentatonic Scale

The A minor pentatonic scale is drawn below. The zeros indicate open strings. The root (note which gives the letter name of the scale) is on the fifth string, open. The notes and tablature for the A minor pentatonic scale are written below the diagram. Practice this scale going from low notes to high, and vice versa.

A Minor Pentatonic Scale

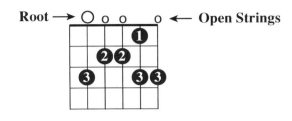

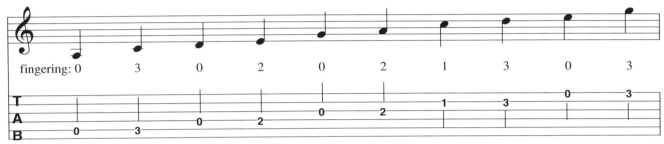

The A minor pentatonic scale can be used to write and improvise solos over Am, A5, and A7 chords. It can also be used to play over all the chords in Blues progressions in the key of A or A minor. Practice playing the following solos, in which all of the notes that are used come from the A minor pentatonic scale. After playing these written solos, write and/or improvise your own solos to the Blues in the key of A or A minor using the minor pentatonic scale.

Blues in A

A Minor Pentatonic Scale

A Minor Shuffle

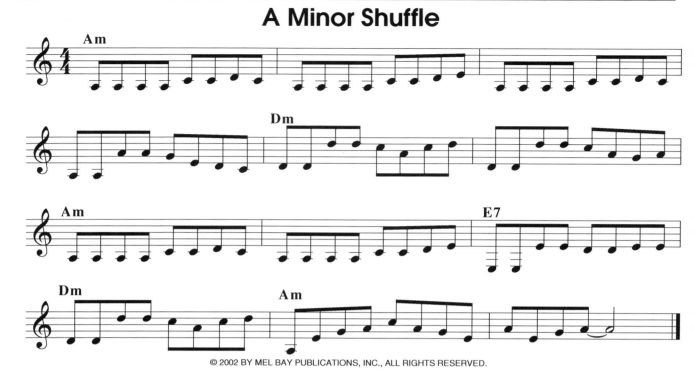

TAB Review
A Minor Blues

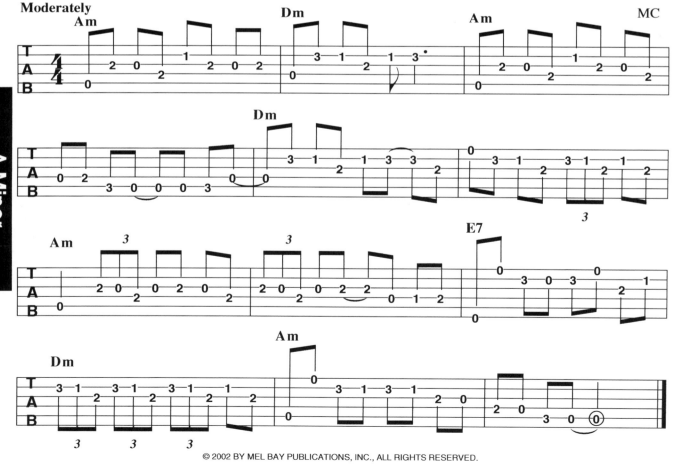

Fingerstyle

"Fingerstyle playing" means playing the strings with the right-hand thumb and fingers, rather than using a pick. Before playing fingerstyle, an understanding of right-hand position and type of strokes is necessary. In the illustration below, the right-hand thumb is to the left of the fingers (when viewed from the top). The thumb is extended and the right-hand fingers are curled. The wrist is bent slightly. To put the right-hand in position, rest the thumb on the fifth string, the index finger on the third string, the middle finger on the second   string,   and the ring finger on the first string.

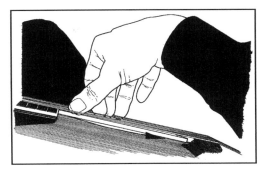

In fingerstyle playing, there are two types of motion used to stroke the strings...free stroke and rest stroke. The free stroke is used to play fingerpicking accompaniment patterns, and the rest stroke is often used when playing single note passages. Free stroke and rest stroke are illustrated and described below.

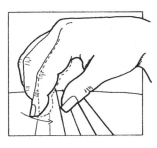
Figure 1

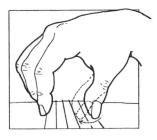
Figure 2

Rest Stroke

The rest stroke is commonly used to play melodies and is popular in solo guitar playing. To do the rest stroke, the flesh on the tip of the finger strokes the string is an upward (not outward) motion. The nail strokes the string as it passes by. *The finger then comes to rest on the next string (see figure 1).* The first joint of the finger (the one closest to the nail) should not bend. The second and third joints are active and should bend.

The thumb rest stroke is done by moving the thumb downward and playing the string with the tip of the thumb and the nail. The thumb then comes to rest on the next string down (see figure 2).

Practice playing the C major scale below and playing each note with the thumb using a rest stroke.

Next, practice the G major scale below playing each note with the right hand index finger using a rest stroke. Now play each note with the right hand middle finger using a rest stroke. Next, play each note with the right-hand third finger using a rest stroke. Finally, play the notes and alternate the middle and index fingers.

Free Stroke

This is the stroke which is commonly used in accompaniment-style fingerpicking. Because it allows the strings to ring. It is good for fingerpicking. It may also be used to play single note melodies. To do the free stroke, the finger picks the string and then is pulled out slightly to avoid touching the next string. Remember, it barely misses the next string. Do not pull away from the guitar too far or the string will slap (see figure 3). As with the rest stroke, when using a free stroke, the first joint should not bend. This first joint acts like a shock absorber. The second and third joints are the active joints.

The free stroke with the thumb is similar. After the thumb strokes the string, it is moved slightly outward to avoid hitting the next string (see figure 4).

Figure 3

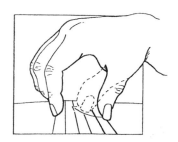

Figure 4

All the fingerpicking patterns and exercises in this section of the book should be done using the free stroke.

The following exercises will develop right-hand coordination which will be helpful in learning fingerpicking patterns. Repeat each exercise several times.

In the following exercises, the numbers written indicate the strings which are to be played (1= 1st string, 2= 2nd string, etc.). The letters, written to the side of the numbers, indicate which right-hand finger is to pick the string.

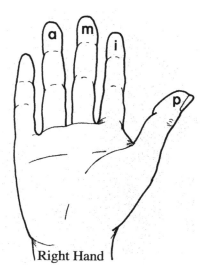

Right Hand

Right Hand
p = pulgar (thumb)
i = índice (index finger)
m = medio (middle finger)
a = anular (third finger, ring finger)

Fingerstyle

In the first exercise, the index finger rests on the 3rd string (touches, but does not play), the middle finger rests on the 2nd string, and the ring finger rests on the 1st string. While the fingers rest on strings one, two, and three, the thumb plays the 6th string open using a free stroke. In all of the exercises below, the strings are played using a free stroke. The stem below each number indicates that each stroke gets one beat.

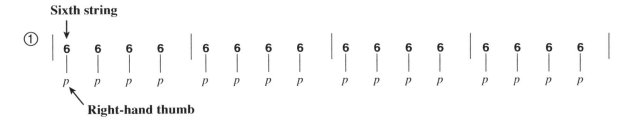

In the next exercises, the thumb rests on the sixth string, while the fingers play strings one, two, and three open.

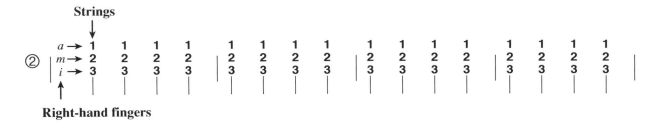

Next, the thumb plays the sixth string at the same time as the fingers play the top strings.

In exercise #4, the thumb alternates with the fingers

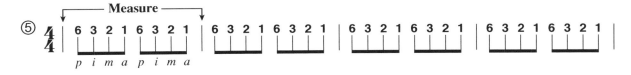

In exercise #5, the thumb plays the 6th string, followed by the index finger playing the 3rd string, the middle finger playing the 2nd string, and the third finger playing the 1st string. The stems under the numbers serve the same purpose as stems on notes. Stems connected with a single beam indicate two strokes (strings picked) per beat (eighth notes). The brackets indicate measures. Each pattern take one, 4/4 measure to complete. The right-hand fingering is written below the string numbers.

Exercise #6 has the finger order as pami, pami, and the string order as 6123, 6123.

Fingerstyle

Fingerpicking Patterns

A fingerpicking pattern which could be used to play songs in 4/4 time is written below. This pattern is for one measure of a 6-string chord in 4/4. Remember, a 6-string chord is one in which when strummed, all six strings are played. Examples of 6-string chords would include G and Em.

The numbers in the pattern below represent strings to be picked. Letters under the numbers show which right-hand fingers are used to pick the string. The rhythm of the pattern is indicated by the stems under the numbers. Hold a G chord and practice this pattern.

6-String Chords (ex. G and Em)

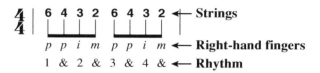

This fingerpicking pattern is sometimes called an "arpeggio-pattern." Arpeggio means "broken chord." In this fingerpicking pattern the chord is "broken" and the strings are played one at a time. This pattern works well with slow songs in 4/4.

The pattern for one measure of a 5-string chord is written below. Notice the right-hand finger order is the same as the pattern for 6-string chords.

In accompaniment style fingerpicking, it is common for the right-hand finger order to remain the same even though the string order may vary.

5-String Chords (ex. C and Am)

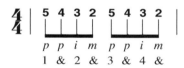

The arpeggio fingerpick pattern for one measure of a 4-string chord is written below.

4-string Chords (ex. D and F)

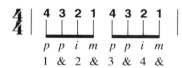

To apply this fingerpick pattern to accompany a song, determine if the chord for the measure is 6-, 5-, or 4-string chord, and then play the appropriate pattern for that chord.

Fingerstyle

Practice the following exercises using the arpeggio fingerpicking pattern. As a guide, the patterns have been written in some of the measures. In the empty measures, play the appropriate pattern for that chord.

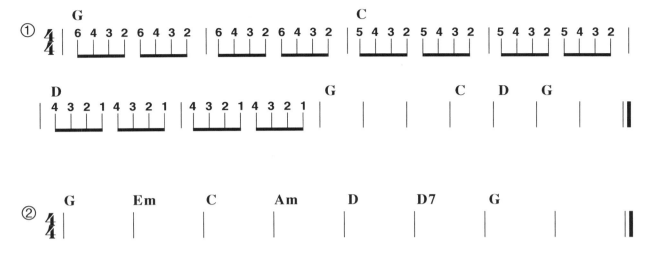

If two chords appear in a measure, half of the pattern is played on each chord.

Practice the following song using the arpeggio fingerpicking pattern. As a help, patterns have been written above some of the measures. Don't be concerned with playing the melody notes. Focus on playing the correct fingerpick pattern.

The Water Is Wide

Fingerstyle

Moveable Minor Pentatonic Scale

Drawn below is a minor pentatonic scale which can be moved up and down the neck. The pattern can begin in any fret. This scale pattern has the "root" on the sixth string. The root is the note which names the scale. The chart below the scale pattern shows the location of the roots on the sixth string. The fret placement of the root determines the letter name of the scale. For example, to play the G minor pentatonic scale, position the pattern so the first finger is on the third fret, sixth string (G). Practice playing the G minor pentatonic scale starting with the first finger on the sixth string, third fret. Play the notes one at a time beginning with the sixth string, first finger, followed by the sixth string, fourth finger. Then, move to the fifth string- first finger- and progress to the first string. Practice this scale pattern beginning the several different frets. Practice playing this scale from low notes to high and vice versa.

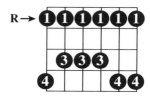

Fret	1	3	5	7	8	10	12
Root name	F	G	A	B	C	D	E

To sharp the scale, move the pattern up one fret. For example, G# minor pentatonic scale begins in the fourth fret. To flat the scale, move it down one fret. For example, Bb minor pentatonic begins the sixth fret.

The following blues solo is in the key of A and uses the notes from the moveable minor pentatonic scale beginning on the sixth string, fifth fret (A). Remember, when a number is on top of another number, play the two strings at the same time.

Summer Blues, Summer Not

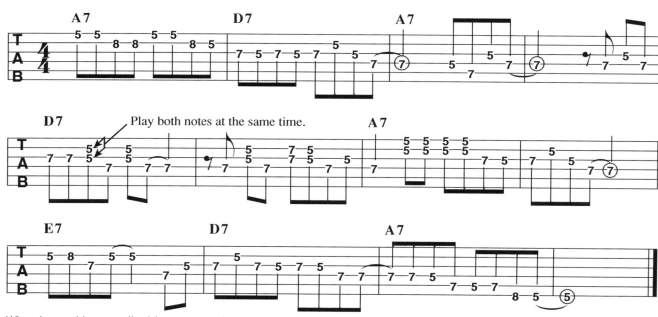

When improvising over the blues progression, any of the notes from the minor pentatonic scale of the key can be used in the solo. The notes must come from the minor pentatonic scale which has the same letter name as the key. Even when the chords in the progression change, the notes used for the solo can come from the scale of the key. For example, when creating an improvised blues solo in the key of A, the notes used in the solo can come from the A minor pentatonic scale. Whether the chords are A7, D7, or E7, the A minor pentatonic scale can be used to play the solo because the entire progression is in the key of A. This rule also applies to blues in a minor key.

Practice creating your own improvised solo to the progression at the top of this page and the blues in the other keys by using the notes from the moveable minor pentatonic scale.

The pattern for the moveable minor pentatonic scale with the root on the fifth string is drawn below. Like the moveable scale pattern with the root of the sixth string, this pattern may be moved up and down the neck. Again, the letter name of the root will determine the letter name of the scale. The chart for the location of the roots on the fifth string is drawn below the scale pattern.

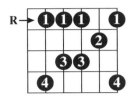

Fret	2	3	5	7	8	10	12
Root name	B	C	D	E	F	G	A

Practice playing the following blues solo in the key of D. All of the notes used in the solo come from the D minor pentatonic scale with the root on the fifth string, fifth fret (D). Notice this solo is 24 measure long. The 12-bar blues form is played twice.

I Know What You Mean

Improvisation

While it is true that any note in the minor pentatonic scale can be used to improvise over a minor, m7, 7th, and 9th chords, some notes will sound better than others. Chord tones are always "safe" notes to play. "Chord tones" are notes which are in the scale, but they are also in the chord for that measure. They sound good because they match the chord being played. These chord tones will sound best if they are placed on strong beats. Harmonically, the strong beats in 4/4 are one and three. In 3/4, the strong beat is beat one. A good technique to practice identifying and playing chord tone is to play a simple solo by using only one note per measure, and make that note be a chord tone. The diagram below shows where the chord tones are in an A7 chord.

The circles show the A minor pentatonic scale and the solid dots show the chord tones. The solid dots which are circled are shortness which are not contained in the scale. Notice that many of the chord tones are found in the scale. The exercise below the diagram shows a simple solo containing only one note per measure, and that note is a chord tone. Because the solos in this section of the book are played up the neck, they will be written in tablature. Most of these solos will be played in the fifth position. This means the left-hand first finger will be used in the fifth fret, the second finger will be used in the sixth fret, the third finger in the seventh fret, and the fourth finger used in the eighth fret. After playing the written exercise, create your own solo using one chord per measure.

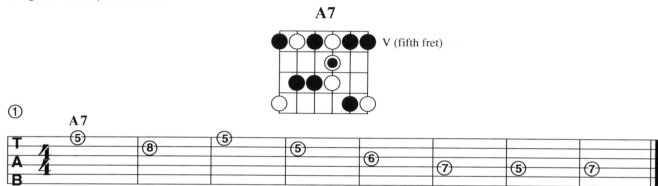

When playing a solo over the blues progression, the same minor pentatonic scale can be used for all three chords in the blues progression. The scale used should have the same letter name as the key of the blues progression. For example, the A minor pentatonic scale can be used for the blues progression in A which contains the chords A7, D7, and E7. Although any note in the scale will work with all three chords, chord tones will sound best. The chord tones for A7 have already been presented. Drawn below are the chord tones foe the D7 and E7 chords. The circles show the A minor pentatonic scale. The solid dots are the chord tones, and the solid, circled dots show chord tones which are not contained in the scale.

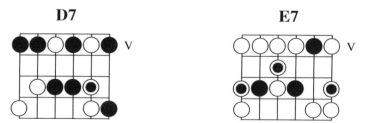

The following 12-bar blues in the key of A solo is comprised of only chord tones from the A7, D7, and E7 chords. After playing the written solo, try creating your own solo using chord tones only.

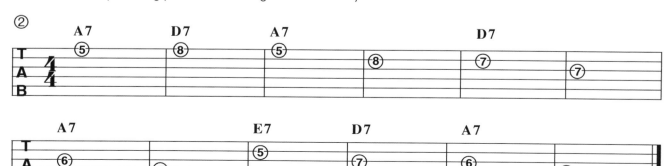

Although it is an excellent exercise, playing only one note per measure can sound a bit dull. The first step in creating interest in the solo is to still play only one note per measure (a chord tone), but repeat the note using an interesting rhythm. Shown below is an excellent rhythm to use first. This rhythm takes one measure in 4/4. Play the same note both times in the measure, and make the note be a chord tone.

count: 1   (2)   &   (3)   4)

The example below is a blues solo using chord tones and the same rhythm in each measure. After playing this solo, create your own solo using different chord tones with this rhythm.

③

Now, rather than playing the same note in each measure, try playing two note in a measure. Still have each note be a chord tone, and use the rhythm which was used in the previous example. The following solo shows how this is done.

④
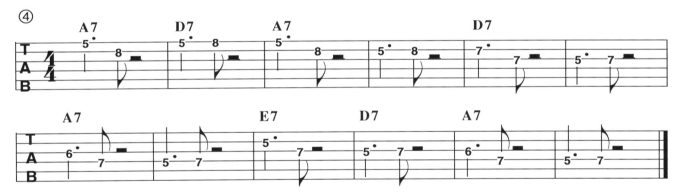

Another rhythm which could be used in show below. It is almost the same as the last rhythm. The difference being that the first note is short. Practice creating a solo using this rhythm.

count: 1   (& 2)   &   (3)   4)

Chord tones are excellent notes to use in a solo. Some chord tones are more popular and sound better than other chord tones. Two popular chord tones to use in a solo are referred to as the seventh and the third. For now, don't be concerned with why they are called the seventh and the third. On the diagrams below, are shown the locations of the seventh and third in the A7, D7, and E7 chords.

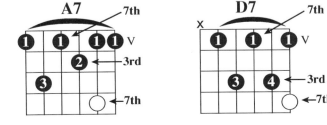
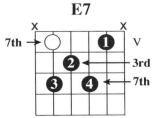

Improvisation

The next solo is made up of only the seventh and the third from each chord. After playing this solo, create your own using sevenths and thirds.

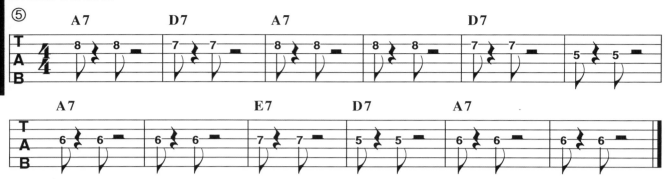

Another good rhythm to practice in the solo is written below.

The following solo uses the new rhythm and chord tones. Notice, that often the seventh from one chord goes to the third of the next chord and vice versa.

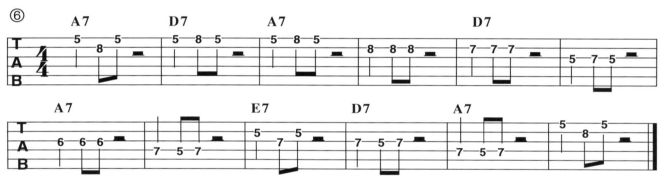

The next step in soloing is to use notes other than chord tones. In the following solo, notice that a chord tone is played on beat one of each measure and sometimes on beat three. The other notes used in the solo come from the A minor pentatonic scale. Also notice that many times the seventh one chord is played followed by the third of the next chord and vice versa. After playing this solo, create you own by using the minor pentatonic scale and chord tones.

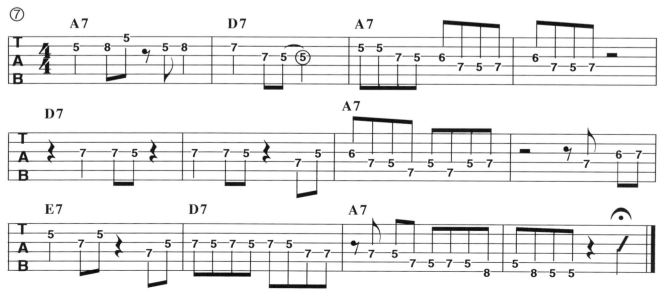

Key of F

In the key of F, there is one flat – B♭. Here is the key signature for the key of F:

Written below is the two octave F major scale. Practice this scale from low notes to high, and then reverse the direction.

Velocity Study

Practice the following piece in the key of F. Remember to flat all of the B notes.

Standing Tall

F Picking Study

Key of F

Etude in F

Flatpick Solo
Moderately fast

The Holly and the Ivy

Flatpick Solo
Gently

Angels We Have Heard on High

Silverheel's Shuffle

The Recital

Guitar Duet
Moderato

MAZAS
Arr. by Mel Bay

Fingerpicking 3/4 Time

This section contains several fingerpicking patterns which work for 3/4 time. The first pattern is similar to the arpeggio fingerpick pattern. The patterns for one measure of the 6-, 5-, and 4-string chords are shown below. The right-hand finger order is written under the string numbers in the 6-string pattern. The same right-hand finger order is used to play each pattern (6-, 5-, and 4-string chords). The rhythm is written under the pattern for the 5-string chords. The rhythm which is played on the 5 string chords is also played on the 6- and 4-string chords.

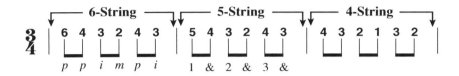

Practice the following exercise using the fingerpick pattern for 3/4.

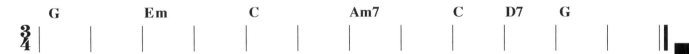

Practice the following song using the fingerpick pattern for 3/4.

Scarborough Fair

Are   you   go-ing   to   Scar-bor-ough   Fair?

Par-sley,   sage,   rose-ma-ry   and   thyme.   Re-

mem-ber   me   to   one   who   lives   there,

She   once   was   a   true   love   of   mine.

The next fingerpick pattern for 3/4 is only slightly different from the first 3/4 pattern presented. In this pattern, on the first beat of each measure, two strings are played together. The lower string is played with the thumb, and the 1st string is played with the right-hand middle finger. Hold any 6-,5-, and 4-string chords and practice this pattern.

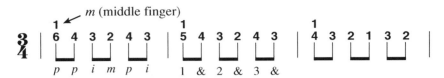

Practice the following exercise and song using this fingerpick pattern.

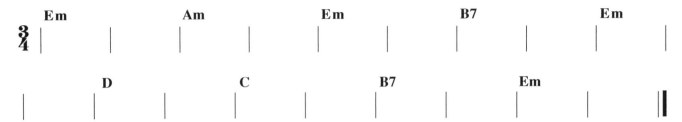

Silent Night

Franz Grüber

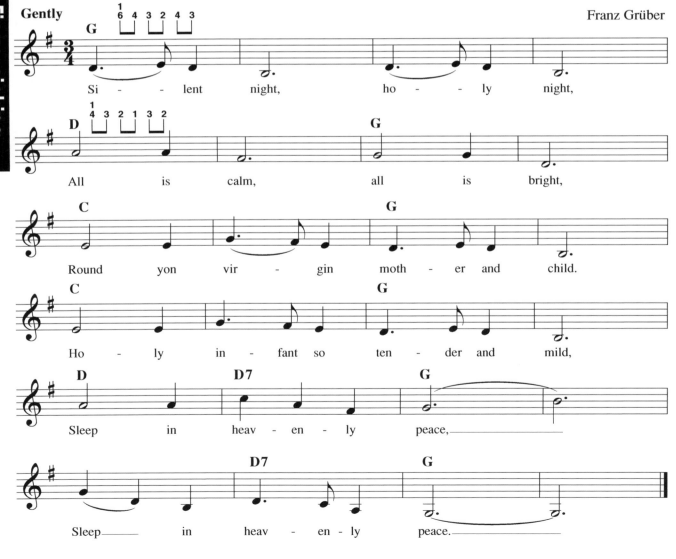

Fingerpicking 3/4 Time

Written below is another fingerpick pattern which works well to play songs in 3/4 time. In this style, when two strings are played together, the index finger (i) plays the lower (larger) string, and the middle finger (m) plays the higher (smaller) string.

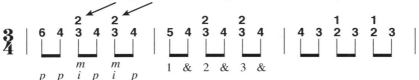

Second string is played with the right-hand middle finger.

Practice the following exercise and song using the new fingerpick pattern for 3/4.

Cmaj7   **Fmaj7**   **Cmaj7**   **Fmaj7**

Am   **G**   **Cmaj7**

Practice playing the previous songs in 3/4 from this section of the book using this new fingerpicking pattern for 3/4 time.

The fingerpick patterns for 3/4 may be played using "swing rhythm." Remember, in swing rhythm, each beat is divided into a one-short pattern rather than divided evenly. Each beat sounds like an eighth note triplet (♪ ♪ ♪) with the middle note tied (♪ ♪). One of the 3/4 fingerpick patterns for 3/4 is shown below with swing rhythm.

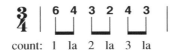

count: 1 la 2 la 3 la

Practice the previous 3/4 songs and exercises in this section of the book, only now use swing rhythm.

Fingerpicking
3/4 Time

Key of D Minor

In the key of D minor, there is one flat – B♭. Because Dm has the same key signature as the key of F major, the key of D minor is "relative" to the key of F major.

D Natural Minor Scale

Picking Study #1

D Harmonic Minor Scale

Notice, in the D harmonic minor scale, the seventh degree (step) of the natural minor scale has been raised 1/2 step. Any natural minor scale can be changed to a harmonic minor scale by raising the seventh degree 1/2 step.

Picking Study #2

D Melodic Minor Scale

In the D melodic minor scale, the sixth and seventh degrees of the natural minor scale have been raised 1/2 step when ascending. When descending, the melodic minor scale is the same as the natural minor scale. Any natural minor scale can be changed to a melodic minor scale by doing this.

Picking Study #3

The following piece is in the key of D minor and is in 6/4 time. In 6/4, there are six beats in a measure, and the quarter note gets one beat.

Fandango

Flatpick Solo

Fast

MC

Key of D Minor

Lady's Fancy

Flatpick Solo
Rousing

WB
Fiddle Tune

Key of D Minor

Canon
from the "Musical Offering"

The second guitarist starts at the end and plays the piece backwards to the beginning. The two parts will harmonize each other.

Allegro

The Rights of Man

Flatpick Solo

Celtic Tune

Medium

Key of D Minor

Rondo

Guitar Ensemble
Allegretto

M. Gebaued, op.10
Arr. by W. Bay

Key change from D to D minor

*High B♭: 1st String – 6th Fret

Key of D Minor

The Slur/ Hammer-on/ Pull-off

A slur is a curved line that connects two or more notes of a different pitch. When a slur occurs, pick only the first note. The remaining notes are fingered, but not picked. A slur going up in pitch is sometimes called a **hammer-on**. With a hammer-on, the second note is sounded by forcefully pushing the left-hand finger on the string. The string is not picked on the second note. A slur going down in pitch is sometimes called a **pull-off**. With a pull-off, the second note is sounded by pulling off the left-hand finger from the first note on an angle. The string is actually picked with the left-hand finger.

Blue Ridge

Caleb's Gorge

Eleven Mile Canyon

Slur/Hammer-on/ 'Pull Off

Travis Fingerpick Style

One of the more popular fingerpick patterns used to play music in 4/4 time is called "Travis picking." This style is named after the great country guitarist, Merle Travis. One of the characteristics of Merle Travis' technique was the thumb alternating between two bass strings. The right hand thumb would play on the first of each beat. The right-hand fingers would play between the thumb strokes. The Travis fingerpick patterns for one measure of 6-string, 5-string, and 4-string chords is shown below. The right-hand finger order is written under the 6-string pattern, and the rhythm is written below the 5-string pattern. The same right-hand finger order and rhythm is used for each pattern. Hold G for the 6-string chord, C for the 5-string chord, and D7 for the 4-string chord, and play the following patterns.

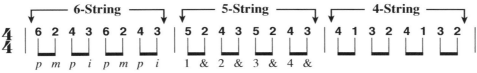

Practice the following exercise using the Travis fingerpick style.

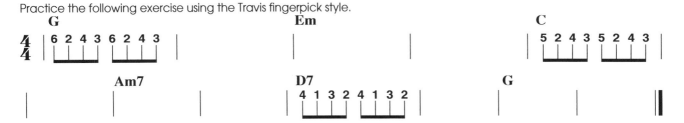

Practice the following songs using the Travis fingerpick style.

A Poor Wayfaring Stranger

Travis Fingerpick Style

Worried Man Blues

Traditional

A variation of the Travis style is written below. It is similar to the Travis pattern previously presented. However, the string which was picked on the "and" of the first beat has been omitted. Hold G,C, and D7 chords and practice this variation.

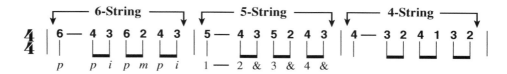

Practice the next exercise using the variation of the Travis pick.

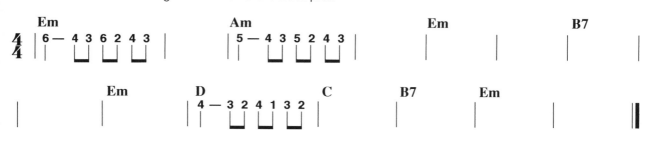

Travis Fingerpick Style

Practice the following songs using the Travis variation

Baby Don't Love Me

You're the Cure

Travis Fingerpick Style

Introduction to Barre Chords

A "barre chord" is a chord in which the first finger of the left hand lays (bars) across five or six strings. As a preparation to playing barre chords, practice the following sequence.

First, hold a DM7 chord (barre the first three strings in the second fret). Strum four strings, four times. Then, strum the first four strings open four times. Repeat this three times as shown below. The loop above the numbers indicates a bar finger. In the beginning, to assist in getting a clean sound from the barre (index) finger, you may want to place the left-hand second finger on top of the first finger to help push. This can be done with exercises 1–8.

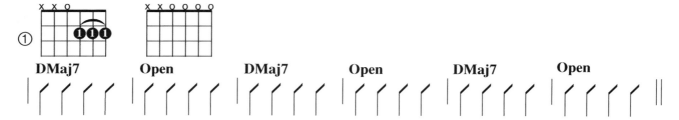

In the next exercise, the chord shape from the previous exercise is moved up and down the neck. Practice this exercise strumming each chord the number of times indicated.

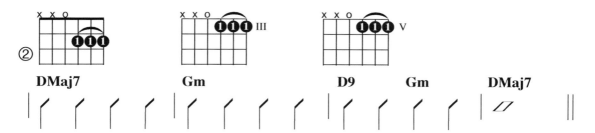

Next, play an A6 chord by barring the first four strings in the second fret. Strum the A6 four times, then strum the first four strings open four times. Repeat the sequence three times.

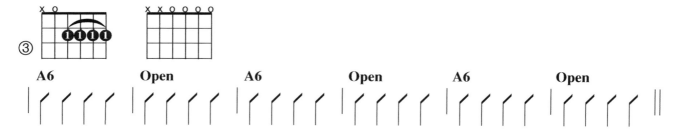

The next exercise uses the same chord form as the previous exercise. The same chord shape is moved up and down the neck. Strum each chord as indicated.

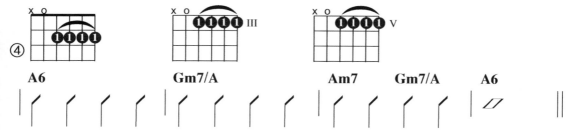

Now play a B11 chord by barring strings 1-5 in the second fret. Strum five strings, four times, then strum five strings open. Repeat the sequence three times.

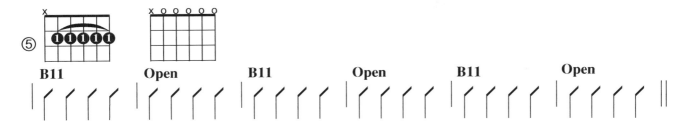

The next exercise has the B11 chord shape moving up and down the neck. Strum as indicated.

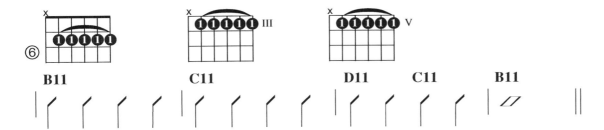

Next, play an F#m7sus chord by barring all six strings in the second fret. Strum the F#m7sus chord by barring all six strings in the second fret. Strum the F#m7sus four times, followed by strumming all six strings open four times. Repeat the sequence three times.

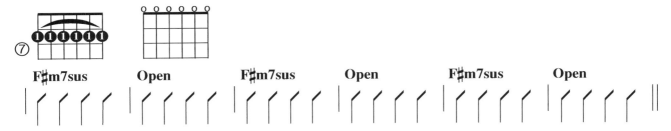

Finally, practice moving the full barre up and down the next as indicated.

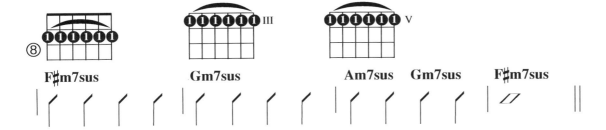

Barre Chords

Bm and F#m Barre Chords

After playing the previous exercises, it is time to learn barre chords in which other fingers are used in addition to the bar finger. Two popular barre chords are F#m and Bm. Because these two barre chords can be built upon open chords, they make an excellent choice for the first barre chords to be learned. To learn the F#m and Bm barre chords, follow the steps outlined below.

F# Minor

A popular barre chord is F#m. To build this chord, play E minor by fingering it with fingers three and four as indicated below. E minor is normally played with fingers two and three. For this exercise, use fingers three and four.

Now, move fingers three and four up to the fourth fret.

Next, leave fingers three and four in the fourth fret and barre the first finger across all six strings in the second fret. This is the barre F#m.

Practice strumming F#m several times, then move the pattern up and down the neck as in the exercise below. Notice the letter name of the chord changes as the pattern is moved up the neck. The formula for determining chord letter names will be given later.

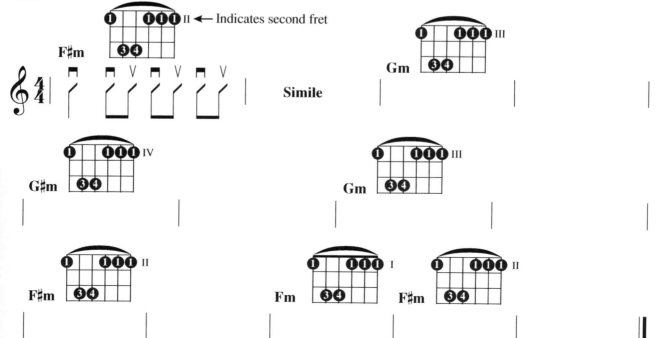

To learn the Bm barre chord, first, play the simple Am chord drawn below.

Am

Next, modify the simple Am chord by changing the fingering as shown below.

Am

Now, move fingers two, three, and four up two frets as shown below.

Finally, leave fingers two, three, and four in the same position as the chord drawn above, and lay the first finger across five strings in the **second fret**. The resulting chord is a barre Bm chord.

Bm

After playing the barre Bm chord, practice moving the pattern up and down the neck as in the exercise below. Notice the letter name of the chord changes as the pattern moves. The formula for locating other minor chords will be given later.

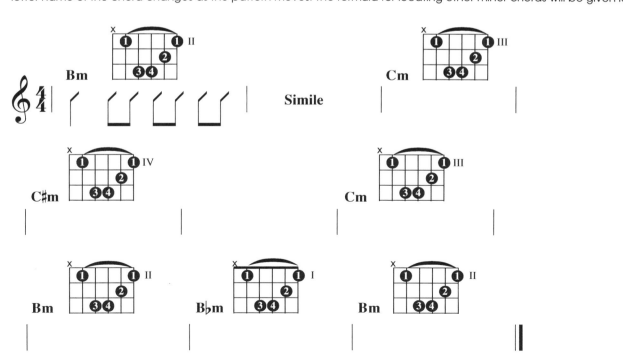

Practice the next exercise, which changes back and fourth from the barre F#m to the barre Bm.

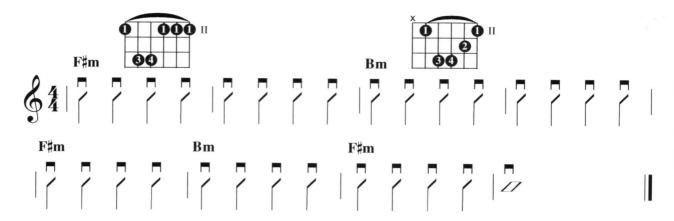

In the following exercise, the barre F#m and Bm chords are used. The A, D, and E7 chords are open chords.

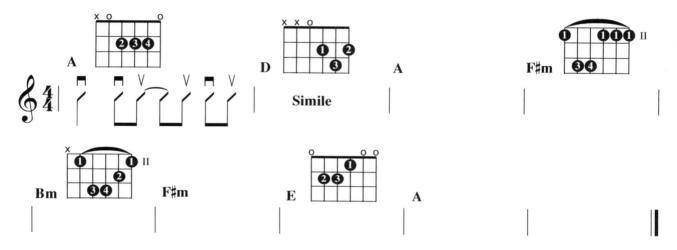

Practice strumming the following song which contains F#m and Bm barre chords. Use the strum pattern written above the first measure to play each measure.

Shenandoah

Anon.

Oh, Shen-an-doah, I long to hear you, A - way, _____ you roll-ing

riv - er. _____ Oh Shen-an-doah I long to hear you, A -

way, _____ we're bound a - way, 'Cross the wide Mis - sou - ri.

Barre Chords

Barre Chords

The information contained in this portion of the "Mastering the Guitar/Class Method" will make it possible to build dozens of chords. Knowing how barre chords work will enable you to play the chords in any key, especially those keys that contain chords which are sharp or flat. Knowing how to play barre chords will also help you to play more complex chords rather than just the basic major and minor chords. Although any chord can be played as a barre chord, you will want to use them primarily on the chords which have a sharp or flat in the name of the chord. In this book, you will be shown two categories of barre chords: those which have the roots on the sixth string, and those which have roots on the fifth string. Knowing the barre chord patterns will make it possible for you to play hundreds of chords.

> **Because the material in this section of the book may be more difficult to play than the other sections, you may want to practice only a portion of it and then move ahead. Then, keep coming back until you have the barre chords mastered.**

First Category

The following diagrams show barre chord patterns from the first category. These chords have their roots (note which names the chord) on the sixth string. All six strings can be strummed or fingerpicked with these chords. In the chart above the diagrams, the numbers show in which fret to place the barre finger. The letters show what the letter name of the chord will be when the bar finger is placed in that fret. The diagrams show the fingerings for the various types of chords (i.e., minor, 7th, etc.). Major chords are those which have only letter names (A, D, F, etc.). Major chords may also be sharp or flat.

Sixth String Roots

Fret	1	3	5	7	8	10	12
Root (chord letter name)	F	G	A	B	C	D	E

Loop indicates bar finger

| (Major) | m (Minor) | 7 (Seventh) | m7 (Minor Seventh) |

To find a barre chord using the chart and the diagrams, do the following: First, place the barre finger in the fret number which corresponds to the root name (letter name) of the chord you're trying to play (A7 would have the barre finger in the fifth fret because the root for A is in the fifth fret, on the sixth string); then, hold the pattern for the type of chord you want to play (major, minor, 7th, etc.). To sharp a barre chord, move the entire pattern up one fret. To flat a barre chord, move the pattern down one fret.

G#m7 would be played like the diagram below. G#m7 is in the fourth fret because the root for G# is in the fourth fret. The fingering for a minor seventh chord is used.

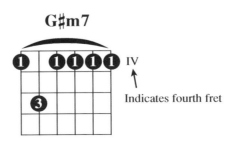

G#m7

IV ← Indicates fourth fret

Practice the following progressions using barre chords only from the first category. In actual playing, many of these chords would not be played as barre chords, but to help you learn barre chords, play all of these chords as barre chords. First, strum down four times in each measure. Then, use strumming or fingerpicking accompaniment patterns which can be used in 4/4.

Second Category

By knowing two categories of barre chords, chord changes may be kept close and more convenient. Also, many times only one or two chords in a song will be played as barre chords. The other chords will be open chords. By knowing two categories of barre chords, the barre chord can be played in frets close to the open chords.

The second category of barre chords has the root on the fifth string. When playing these chords, five strings are strummed or fingerpicked. In the chart above the diagrams, on the next page, the numbers show in which fret on the fifth string to place the bar finger. The letters show what the letter name (root) of the chord will be when the bar is placed in that fret. As with the first category of barre chords, to sharp a barre chord, move the entire pattern up one fret and to flat a barre chord, move the entire pattern down one fret. The diagrams on the next page show the fingerings for the various types of chords. Because the root for D would be in the fifth fret, the D7 chord would be played like this:

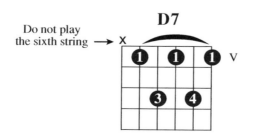

Because the root is on the fifth string, the second category of barre chords will generally sound best if only five strings are strummed.

Fifth String Roots

Fret	2	3	5	7	8	10	12
Root (chord letter name)	B	C	D	E	F	G	A

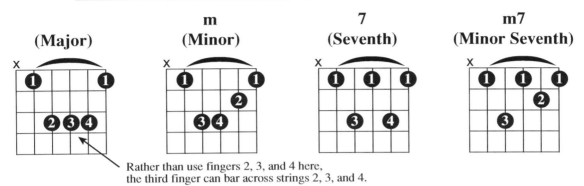

Rather than use fingers 2, 3, and 4 here, the third finger can bar across strings 2, 3, and 4.

The same process is used in finding these chords as was used in finding the position and fingering for the barre chords with the roots on the sixth string. For example, if you wanted to find a C#m7 chord, place the barre finger on the fourth fret because the C# root is on the fifth string fourth fret (C is in the third fret and to sharp it you move it up one fret), then hold the pattern for a m7 chord. So a C#m7 chord would be played like this:

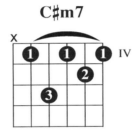

If you use alternating bass or fingerpicking accompaniment patterns with barre chords from the second category, play them as five-string chords.

Practice the following progressions using only barre chords from the second category. Play all of the chords in these progressions as barre chords. Use strum patterns or fingerpick patterns for 4/4.

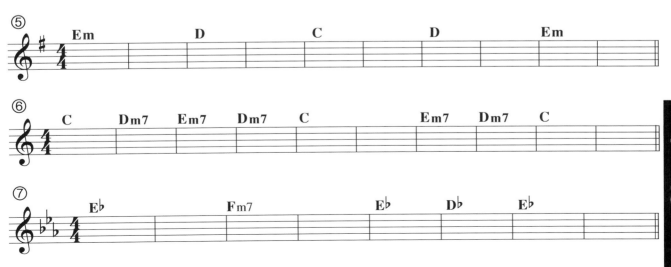

Knowing two categories of barre chords will make your chord changes more convenient. For example, if you are playing an F#m and the next chord is Bm, it would be best to play F#m in the second fret using the first category of barre chords, and then play Bm in the second fret using the second category as drawn below. Otherwise, Bm would be in the seventh fret using the first category. Going from the second fret to the seventh fret is not nearly as convenient as staying in the second fret.

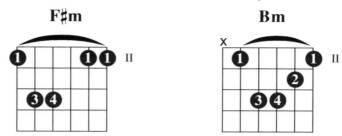

Practice the following progressions using barre chords from both categories. You may have to figure out both ways of playing a barre chord and then using the one which is closest to the chords you just played. Play all of the chords in these progressions as barre chords. Use strum and/or fingerpick patterns for 4/4 or 3/4 depending on the time signature.

In "real life" playing, it would be rare that all of the chords to a song would be played as barre chords, especially if you are playing acoustic guitar. If you have a choice of playing Am as an open chord or as a barre chord, use the open chord. Again, a good clue that a chord is to be played as a barre chord, is the presence of a sharp or flat sign. In the following progressions, the circled chords should be played as barre chords. The chords which are not circled should be played as open chords. Practice the progressions first using only down strums, then use strum or fingerpick accompaniment patterns. Practice changing smoothly from the open chords to the barre chords.

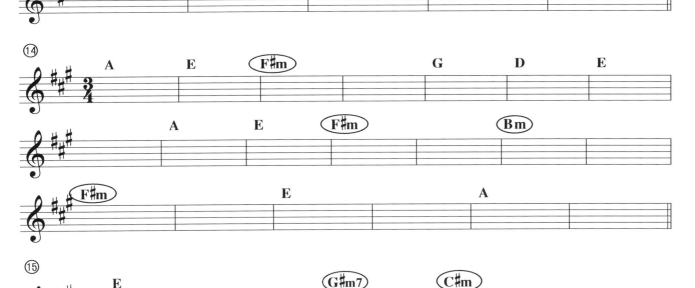

Portraits of Spain
Guitar I
(Conductor's Score Found on Page 157)

Portraits of Spain

Portraits of Spain
Guitar II
(Conductor's Score Found on Page 157)

MC

Portraits of Spain

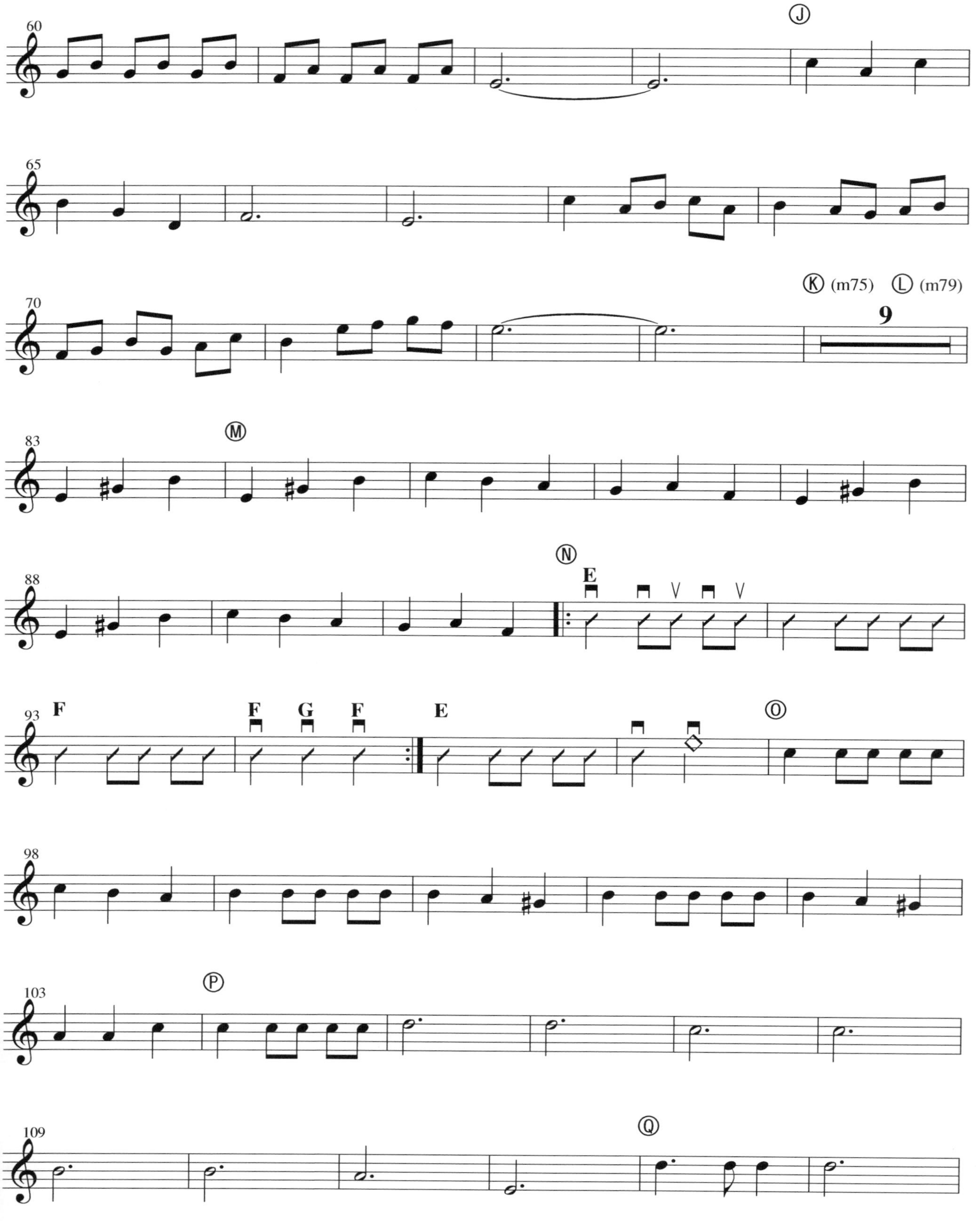
60
J
65
70
K (m75) L (m79)
9
83
M
88
N
E
93
F
F G F
E
O
98
103
P
109
Q

Portraits of Spain
Guitar III
(Conductor's Score Found on Page 157)

Portraits of Spain

Portraits of Spain
Guitar IV
(Conductor's Score Found on Page 157)

MC

Portraits of Spain

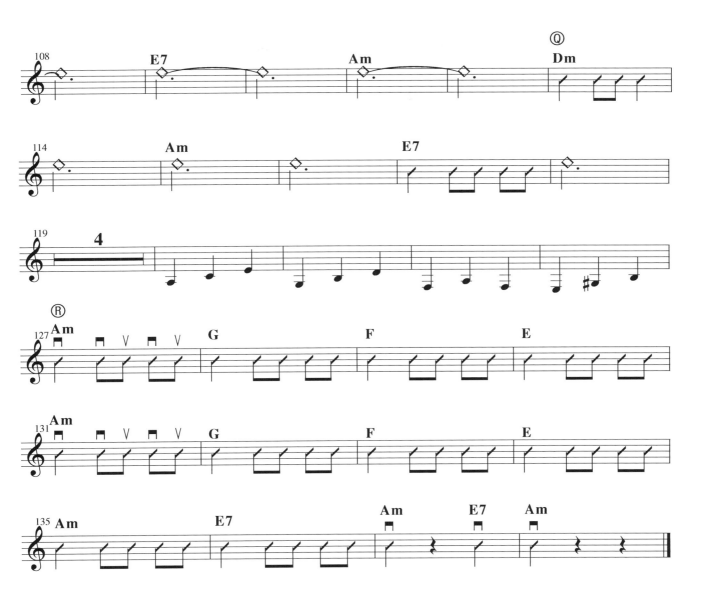

Playing Two or More Notes Together

(Pickstyle)

Double Stops/ Triads

When two or more notes are written on top of each other, play the notes at the same time. This is called a **double stop**. Figure out the placement of the notes, beginning with the top note, and play the notes quickly so they sound at the same time.

Double Stop Study I

Double Stop Study II

If two notes appear to be played on the same string, such as the B and D shown below, the lower note is moved to the next lower string. The circled number next to the note indicates the string on which the lower note is to be played. In the example below, the lower note (B) is played on the third string, fourth fret. The left-hand fingers are given with the number to the left of the notes.

3rd String, 4th Fret

Trading Places

Greensleeves

The E note is played
2nd string, 5th fret.

Triads

The *triad* is a chord which contains three notes. Figure out the placement of all three notes (beginning with the top note) and
play them at the same time.

WB

Minor Song

WB

The Clock

Moderately

WB

Echoes

Smoothly

WB

Open String

Arpeggio Picking

Flowing

WB

Chimes

Medium, Gently

WB

Upper Notes on the First String

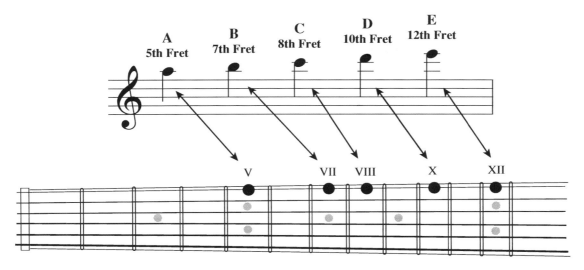

Play the following song in which all of the notes are played on the first string. Notice the left-hand fingerings.

Málaga

Late Spring

Carol of the Bells

Guitar I

Guitar Ensemble – Guitar I   ♩=138   (Conductor's Score Found on Page 161)

Carol of the Bells

Guitar II

(Conductor's Score Found on Page 161)

Carol of the Bells

Guitar III

(Conductor's Score Found on Page 161)

Carol of the Bells
Guitar IV
(Conductor's Score Found on Page 161)

Guitar Ensemble – Guitar IV

Carol of the Bells

Hip Hop #49
Guitar I
(Conductor's Score Found on Page 163)

Hip Hop #49

Hip Hop #49

Guitar II

(Conductor's Score Found on Page 163)

Hip Hop #49

Hip Hop #49
Guitar III
(Conductor's Score Found on Page 163)

Hip Hop #49
Guitar IV
(Conductor's Score Found on Page 163)

Play these B notes on the
3rd string, fourth fret.

Block Chords

When more than three notes are played together, the chord that results is called a **block chord**. Block chords can contain four, five, or six notes. As with triads, play the notes quickly so they sound at the same time.

Practice the following pieces which contain **double stops**, **triads**, and **block chords**.

Spanish Romance

Black Is The Color of My True Love's Hair

Music in Two Parts

Playing "music in two parts" means that the right-hand thumb will play one part and the right-hand fingers will play another part. Occasionally, the fingers and/or the thumb will use the rest stroke. In most of the pieces and exercises in this section of the book, the free stroke will be used. For a review of rest stroke and free stroke see p. 76-77.

Playing Two Parts Together

Generally, when music for the guitar is written in two parts, the thumb plays the notes which have the stems going down and the fingers play the notes with the stems going up. Each part (the fingers and the thumb) contains the correct number of beats to complete the measure. Therefore, the thumb part may have a rest while the fingers are playing and vice versa.

Practice the following solos playing the upper notes (with the stems going up) with the fingers, and playing the lower notes (with the stems going down) with the thumb. When the notes line up, play them together. Notice the right-hand fingers alternate. You may want to practice the top notes alone, and then add the thumb.

Hey, Watch This

Two-Part Study in E Minor

In this piece, the chords are written above the measures for another guitarist to play an accompaniment. Do not hold the chords while playing the solo.

Music in Two Parts

Study In A Minor

③

Two Parts at 1:30

④

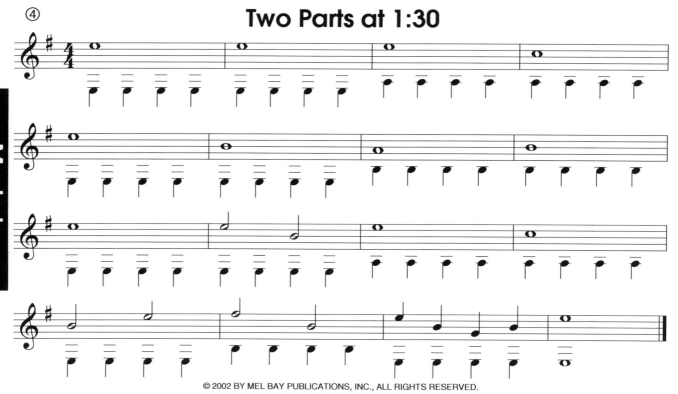

A Soalin'

⑤

Suggested right-hand fingers

Suggested left-hand fingers

Music in Two Parts

Two-Part Estudio

The Plot Thickens

Music in Two Parts

Practice the following solo with the thumb playing the lower notes and the finger playing the higher notes.

Trev and Tom

Play the following arrangement of "Greensleeves." be sure to hold the bass note (low note) for its total time value. A finger may have to be holding a bass note and allowing it to ring while the melody (upper note) is moving.

Letters by notes indicate which right-hand finger to use when picking the string. Numbers indicate left-hand fingers and a circled number indicates the string on which that note is to be played.

Greensleeves

Music in Two Parts

The following solo in two parts is written in tablature. The same rules for fingering apply. The numbers in parenthesis are suggested left-hand fingers. Notice the right-hand a-m-i pattern is used on each triplet played with the right-hand fingers. In measures five and six, barre the left-hand first finger across the first three strings in the fifth fret.

The Hidden Castle

MC

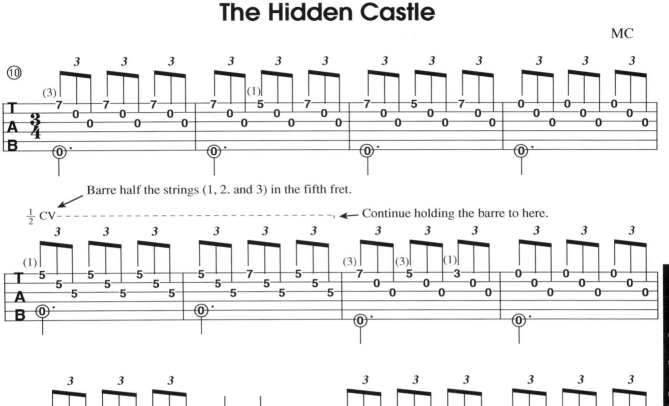

Barre half the strings (1, 2. and 3) in the fifth fret.

½ CV -- ← Continue holding the barre to here.

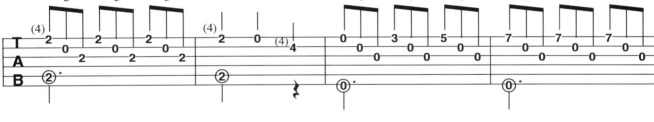

Music in Two Parts

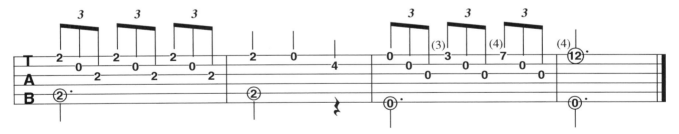

If the stems go down and up on a note, the note is played with the thumb, but is connected rhythmically to the other notes connected to it. The note with the stem going down gets 1/2 beat, but it is allowed to ring for two beats. It is as though there are two notes played at the same time (an eighth note and a half note).

In the following piece, allow all the notes in each measure to ring through each other. Accent the thumb strokes.

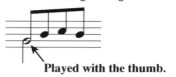

Played with the thumb.

Practice the following solo in which some of the notes have double stems. Use free stroke.

Estudio

D. Aguado

Mexican Lament

Music in Two Parts

Ashley's Song

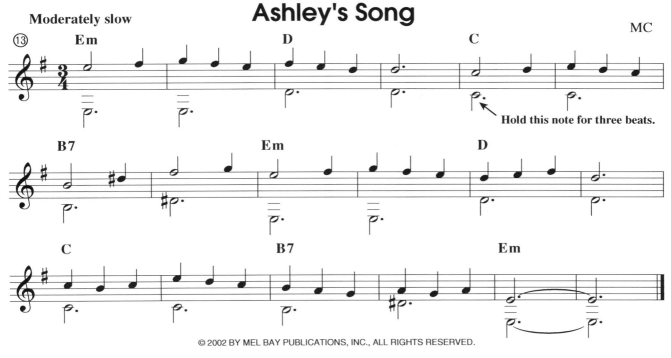

Hold this note for three beats.

Fingerpicking Solos

O Come, O Come Emmanuel

Make sure these notes ring for two beats.
Do not lift the left-hand finger too early.

Fingerpicking Solos

A Knight's Wish

Swingin' the Changes

MC

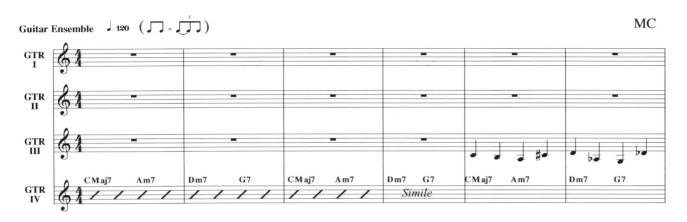

Swingin' the
Changes

Swingin' the Changes

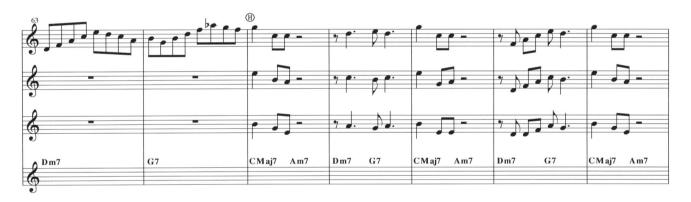

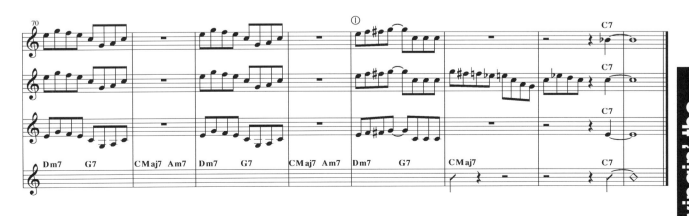

Swingin' the Changes

Acoustic Blues

Guitar Ensemble ♩ = 92

MC

Acoustic Blues

Portraits of Spain

MC

Portrait's of Spain

Carol of the Bells

Carol of the Bells

Hip Hop #49

Hip Hop #49

Note Review

String		Frets				
	0	**1**	**2**	**3**	**4**	**5**
6	E	F	F# or Gb	G	G# or Ab	
5	A	A# or Bb	B	C	C# or Db	
4	D	D# or Eb	E	F	F# or Gb	
3	G	G# or Ab	A	A# or Bb		
2	B	C	C# or Db	D	D# or Eb	
1	E	F	F# or Gb	G	G# or Ab	A

Note Review

Chord Review

G
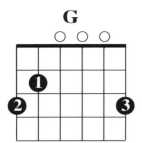

C
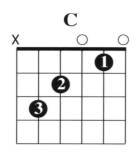

G7
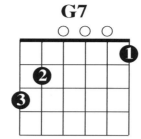

Em
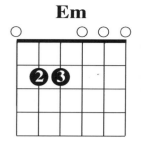

D
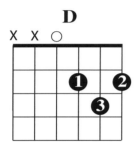

Am
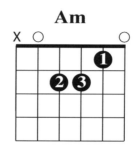

D7
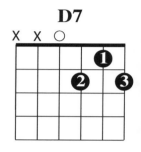

A7
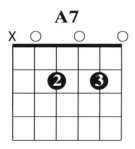

E7
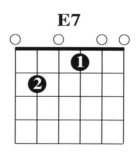

B7
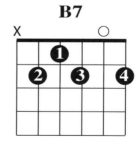

Bm
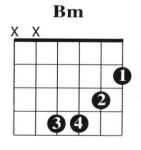

F
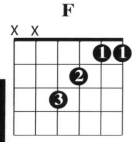

C7
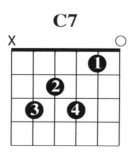

B♭
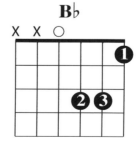

Dm
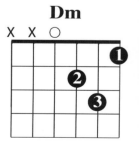

Chord Review

16

Made in the USA
Lexington, KY
13 September 2011